FANTASTIC FS

How to make the most ama　　　　nators

2nd

Ann Morse-Brown

Author and Series Editor: Ann Morse-Brown, formerly Course Director
of the Wombourne School of Millinery. The School closed in 2007 and the
content of all the courses is now available in ebook or hard copy format
from www.how2hats.com. In addition many more courses worldwide are
listed at www.hatcourses.com
Design & Production: Morse-Brown Design Limited
www.morsebrowndesign.co.uk
Published by Morse-Brown Publishing
For more titles in this series, see **www.how2hats.com**
Copyright © 2010 Ann Morse-Brown
ISBN 978-1-907615-02-3

Fantastic feathers

Feathers are fascinating! Beautiful on the bird, they are also wonderful to wear as 'Fascinator' hats or made into adornments for wedding or race-going hats. Not only this, they can be mounted onto pins as brooches or corsages or fixed on bags and belts or even added to masks to wear to the ball. Your imagination will be fired by amazing possibilities as you read on...

We show you the secrets of changing just a few kinds of ordinary feathers gleaned from domestic birds into the most exotic kind of head-piece which looks as if it cost a million dollars! Find out how to dye feathers to just the colour you need to match an outfit or hand bag: how to combine them with fabrics – even how to make a tiny 'cocktail' hat as a base which will show them off to perfection.

No special equipment is needed, just a little time and some things you have around the house already. We tell you where to get the feathers and dyes you will need – maybe you even have some already – so create a space and prepare to start your masterpiece!

This book is written in an easy-to-follow style, with step-by-step photographs of every stage. In it you will meet Beth, who taught these techniques to students from all over the world while she was principal tutor at the Wombourne School of Millinery in the UK. At the end of the book, by way of inspiration, you will meet some of these students and be able to admire the lovely pieces they made.

We do suggest that you read the book all the way through before you start, to give yourself an overview, and to make sure that you have all the equipment to hand for the project.

Caution: Some dyes contain poisonous heavy metals and should not be allowed to come into contact with your skin. Rubber gloves are essential! It is also advisable to wear eye protection at all times. Always observe the safety instructions on the containers of the materials that you will be using.

You will need:

A selection of feathers: natural and white, bleached and unbleached – see details, page 6. A good selection of natural feathers is available from **www.parkin-fabrics.co.uk**

Jacquard acid dyes (produced by Rupert, Gibbon & Spider, Inc, Healdsburg, CA 95448, USA. Available in the UK from **www.millinerwarehouse.com**)

For suppliers in other parts of the world, check the millinery supplies link on the How2hats website: **www.how2hats.com**

A useful selection of basic dye colours for mixing is:
Brilliant blue
• Yellow sun
• Scarlet
• Ecru

Useful additions to the range are:
• Violet
• Gold Ochre
• Salmon
• Pink
• Black

Then you will need the following items:

• Colour wheel for help in colour mixing. You can find one on the internet or in any good art book. Or if you have an iPhone try this app: **http://bit.ly/colourwheel**
• Hotplate, electric or gas, with heat control
• Old saucepans, which you should keep exclusively for dyeing and not use again for food
• Plastic drinks cups, the type that can take boiling water (discard after use)
• Plastic knives, which make useful and inexpensive tools for measuring out and stirring dyes
• Masking tape
• Waterproof apron
• Plastic safety glasses, with side shields
• Plastic table covering to protect your work surface
• Plastic tongs (suitable for use in boiling water)
• Steam iron and ironing board
• Disposable rubber gloves
• Hairdryer with slow and fast speeds
• Hair curling tongs – different sizes are useful, especially when working with larger feathers
• Bleach – the thin, household variety
• Shallow container large enough to immerse feathers in – glass or other non-metallic material

- An old pillowcase or other thin fabric bag to hold feathers for drying in quantity
- Covered millinery wire.
- Pliers and wire cutters
- Silver and/or gold wire – one 50 gram pack 0.04 / 0.03mm (approx 34 gauge)
- Crimp beads – 1 pack of 100 – available from **www.fredaldous.co.uk**
- Beads – a selection of various kinds. (optional)
- Alice bands (hair bands), covered and clear, wide and narrow
- Hot-melt glue gun and glue sticks
- Bias binding (tape), white or natural
- Fabric strips cut on the bias for binding. Preferably satin, or you can use cotton or silk. White or natural
- A small piece of polystyrene (Styrofoam) for holding wired feathers and beads while you work (optional)
- Old towels
- Paper towel
- Sewing threads in a range of colours
- Uhu or other quick-drying glue

The following items should be added to the list, if you wish to create sinamay bases for your feather mounts:

- 0.5 yard/metre veiling (optional)
- Polystyrene (Styrofoam) display head. Note that this is not designed for shaping hats on and pins may damage it. It can however be used a few times for 'blocking', then discarded
- Cling film (saran wrap) or thin plastic sheet
- Spray bottle
- PVA (white) craft glue (known as 'Elmers' in the USA)
- Measuring spoons
- Small bowl
- Household paint brush
- Pieces of sinamay – 0.5 yard/metre is enough to create a base and binding. Smaller pieces can be used to create bases which can be bound with other fabrics
- Satin bias binding (tape), or pieces of silk to create bias binding
- Long ruler (36"/1m)
- 0.5 yard/metre spring steel millinery wire
- Glass-headed dressmaker's pins
- Chinagraph pencil or tailor's chalk
- Sewing machine (optional)
- Long, strong (darning) needle
- Comb and ribbon for binding (colour to match sinamay)
- Old toothbrush
- White vinegar, small amount.

Feathers we will use

This is not an exhaustive list – there are many others which could be used. Once you have experimented with some of the ones we show, you will have confidence to try using others.

Chicken
- Hackle – these come from the neck (neck hackle) or from the hip of the cockerel
- Coque (often simply Coq, pronounced 'coke') – this is the tail feather of the cockerel and lengths can be from 4 to 14 inches (10 to 36 cm)
- Natural coque – these are known more commonly as 'bronze' or 'chinchilla'
- Stripped coque – these are the tail feathers of the cockerel. The bottom part of the feather has been stripped on both sides to leave a small part of the feather at the tip.

All these feathers come in a number of natural shades.

Turkey (not shown in picture)
- Marabou – These are from the hip of the turkey, and are extremely soft & fluffy
- Flats – these can be made into arrowheads by stripping.

Goose
- Spiky goose – this is the narrow part of the pointer feather. The narrow side is stripped to the base.

Guinea Fowl
- These feathers are all quite small, with beautiful markings.

Illustrated – clockwise from top left: Stripped coq (or coque) feathers in two lengths; an example of a small ostrich feather, partially stripped; Biot, or Spiky goose feathers – these come loose as pictured or strung together, like the coq feathers; Guinea fowl feathers, strung; Hackle feathers, strung.

Dyes

The illustration below shows a selection of the Jacquard acid dyes we use. Although they are called 'acid' dyes, they do not become acidic until a small amount of vinegar (acid) is added to the dye mixture when boiling. The colours are brilliant and fast: ½ an ounce (14 grams) of dye will colour approx 2 lbs (1 kilo) of fabric – that's a lot of feathers! Note the table covering to protect the surface. Beside the dyes is a selection of feathers to begin experimenting with.

Techniques

1. Dyeing & drying

From the selection of dyes that you have obtained, you can mix a wide variety of different colours. At this stage in the course, Beth talks to the students about the use of the colour wheel, which classifies the colours in 'families' and gives you an idea of what to expect when you mix various colours together. Our pictures show both sides of the wheel.

Pale or low intensity colours can be produced by simply dissolving some dye in boiling water, but deeper or more intense colours can be obtained by adding vinegar to the mixture and boiling.

Front of colour wheel

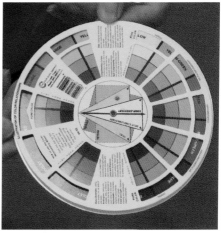

Reverse of colour wheel

Start by pouring a small amount of boiling water into a separate plastic cup for each colour that you want to mix. (Remember – use boiling water-resistant cups!) Bear in mind that this will produce low intensity colours, but you will be able to check that you have the correct colour before going on to the next stage where you increase the intensity to produce the value that you want. We would like to create a green, so begin here with a small amount of blue dye.

We find a plastic knife useful for taking the powdered dye from the pot, and for stirring. Use a separate knife for each colour, and another to stir the mixture.

We stir the blue into the boiling water (1). Now add an equal or slightly smaller amount of yellow to the cup (2).

When you are working with the dye, wear protective rubber gloves. Some dyes contain heavy metals which can penetrate the skin and cause harm.

The new colour is apparent now. Time to add some feathers and see what we have achieved. Beth selects some hackle feathers and swishes them around in the dye (3). They take a few moments to 'take' the dye as feathers contain a natural grease. She perseveres with moving them about in the dye until this is overcome. When wet they look a bit bedraggled, but they have taken the colour well after only a few moments.

The hairdryer, set on cool, will soon restore their beauty (4). Now they look fluffy again. The colour tone seems right.

To keep the feathers in their colour groups and to stop them blowing around, we use masking tape to fix them to the table covering. This means that more feathers can be added, and if care is taken, the tape will not damage the feathers when they are removed for mounting. Here the first hackle and coq feathers are secured (5).

5

Having experimented and created the right colour in the plastic cup, it is time to heat the dye. Heating the mixture with a dash of white vinegar will make the colour considerably more intense.

When the mixture boils, the feathers are added and stirred (6). There is not much liquid in the pan, so it is important to watch it all the time and never leave it unattended.

Remove the feathers when the colour seems to be of the right intensity – a few minutes of boiling may be enough. The longer the feathers are in the boiling liquid, the more intense the colour will be. Put them out onto a piece of paper towel to remove any excess dye as soon as they are ready (7).

Dry them as before, or, if you have a large quantity to dry, speed the process by putting the feathers all together into an old pillowcase or other bag made from thin material. (The kind sold for keeping small items of clothing together in an automatic washing machine could work quite well). Gather the open top around the nozzle of the hairdryer, making sure that the air vents are kept free and the temperature is set to 'cool' (8). For even larger quantities, put the feathers in the pillow case, tie the opening and put it in a tumble dryer.

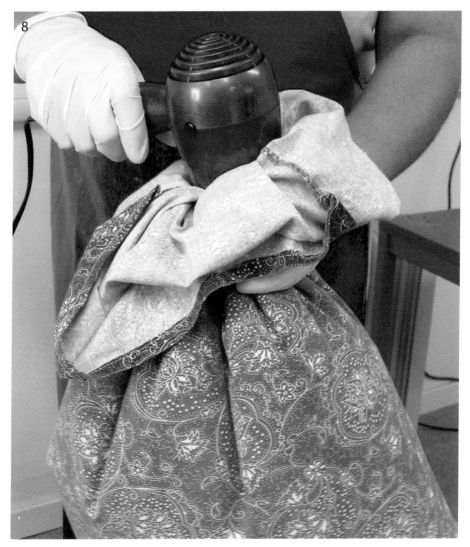

8

The first feathers to be boiled and dried are added to the line of feathers. See how the colour has deepened into a beautiful rich green (9). The colour intensifies if the feathers are boiled in the dye for longer. Experiment to find the tone you need. We now have a selection of colours to work with.

9

2. 'Burning'

Now Beth demonstrates a new technique – that of creating what is known as a 'burnt' feather. The technique alters the look of the feather making it seem less substantial and more delicate and is achieved by immersing feathers in bleach. Use a non-metallic container (plastic or glass) big enough to contain your feather. Wearing rubber gloves, Beth adds an ostrich feather to the bleach and moves it about (10). It takes a few moments for the liquid to penetrate the feather's structure.

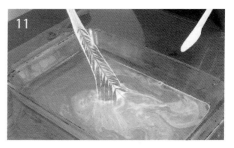

After a few moments, remove the feather (11) and wash the bleach out under the tap (12). Add a little washing-up liquid, drawing it gently along the feather. Finally, rinse away any remaining bleach and liquid by holding it under the cold tap.

Dry. Compare the picture of the original feather with it after 'burning' and see how the character of the feather has changed. Although it now looks quite sparse, it can form a beautiful addition to a design. Brush any tangles out of the feather with a toothbrush (13). The bleach will, of course, also remove any colour from the feather, although it probably won't take out natural markings, just reduce their intensity. If you want to use a burnt feather in your mount, burn it first and dye it later. Burning works well on many feathers and is worth experimenting with.

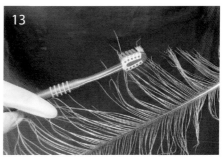

3. Making a feather 'pom'

Ostrich feathers can be used in another attractive way, if the vane, or feathery part is removed from the quill and gathered together in a bunch. This is known as a pom. They are available commercially in different colours, but if you need one to match an outfit or a hat, it is easy to create your own. To make a large pom you will need two large ostrich feathers. If you are going to dye the pom, use white feathers to begin with. Beth demonstrates with one small ostrich feather, just to show the technique. Work in a draught free place or the air will be full of fluff! Grasp a part of the feather at one side and carefully strip it off the quill, laying it gently on the table (14). Take the next part and strip this off the quill too, laying it gently in a separate place. Repeat this on the opposite side of the quill, always putting parts of the same length together. Continue until the feather is completely stripped and you have lots of graded length bunches (15). Note: don't throw away the quill – it can be used in a different arrangement.

Take a length of covered millinery wire, approx. 15 inches (38 cm) and bend it back on itself to make a double thickness. Place the longest bunch close to the folded end of the wire, which will become the centre of the pom (16). Now take a long length of thread, double it and begin to bind the bunch to the wire by winding the thread round the bottom and also round the wire loop, thus drawing bunch and wire together. Bind firmly.

There is no need to make a knot to start the binding, just use a little glue between bindings to help everything to stay in place. Add the rest of the bunches, one at a time, turning the pom so that bunches are added evenly all round. Bind between each addition. Work from the longest bunch to the shortest so that a round form is created. The result is a fluffy ball of delicate softness (17).

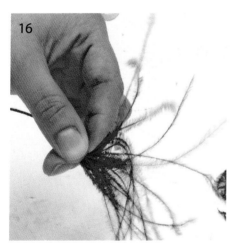

16

17

4. Curling

Feathers can be curled in the same way as hair. Plug in the curling tongs and allow to heat. Beth demonstrates curling a spiky goose. Trap the very end of the feather under the opening prong of the tongs, and wrap the rest of the feather around the closed tongs, being careful that the feather is not squashed (18). Spiky goose feathers are particularly attractive when curled in this way – the curling opens the feather so that it's natural structure can be seen. Beth has also curled some hackle feathers which also look very attractive (19). Larger feathers may need several treatments. Don't try to bend a stiff quill too quickly. Feathers with thick quills may need to be soaked overnight before curling and a curling tongs with a larger diameter used.

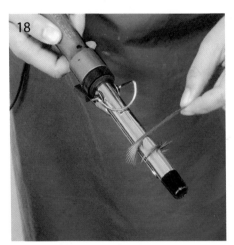

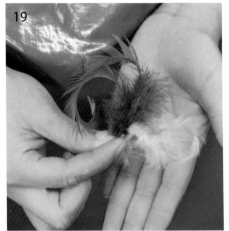

5. Knotting

Another technique particularly suitable for spiky goose feathers is that of knotting. The picture below (20) shows two feathers which have been knotted, together with an unknotted one for contrast. Knotted feathers can add lots of interest to mounts, and can also make a beautiful mount by themselves. See the pictures of finished hats and head pieces at the end of this book. Be careful as you knot the feather not to pull too hard or too quickly, or you will break the quill which is not very strong. Knotting them while they are wet may help.

20

6. Adding length to short feather stems

Some feathers have very short quills which can limit their use somewhat. An example is the guinea fowl feather – they take the dye beautifully while retaining their distinctive markings, but have very short quills.

To create a stem so that they can be used in a wider variety of applications, fix the feather quill to a piece of 'gold' or 'silver' wire with a crimp bead. These are tiny soft metal tubes – see the packet illustrated (21).

Thread the quill into the bead from one direction and the wire in from the other and flatten the bead with the pliers (22). Trim off any excess wire and quill if necessary. Now the feather can be used like a stripped coq, or the wire curved to place the feather wherever it looks attractive in the arrangement.

Another attractive way of adding dimension to an arrangement.

21

22

7. Creating a mount

Now we have a range of feathers in different shades of our chosen colour, we are ready to create a mount. This is an arrangement of feathers and possibly other decorative items which can be used in a variety of ways.

Beth takes a length of covered millinery wire, approx. 15 inches (38 cm) and bends it back on itself to make a double thickness (23). Close to the folded end, she places some feathers. As these will be at the centre of the mount, the tallest of the ones selected are used first.

Beth has chosen some coq feathers to begin with. Using a double thread in an appropriate colour, she binds the feathers to the wire by winding the thread round the quills and wire, to draw them together (24). Bind firmly – use a strong thread if the mount will be large or if the quill is thick. There is no need to make a knot to start the binding: later a little glue will help everything to stay in place. The wire at the core will make the mount much more versatile, enabling it to be curved into an appropriate shape.

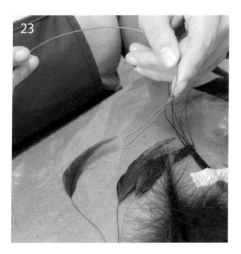

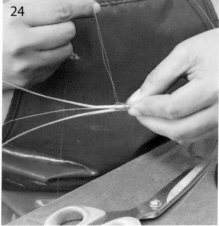

Now Beth adds some hackle feathers and binds again. Some of the wired guinea fowl feathers are added next (25) and are bound onto the wire in the same way (26).

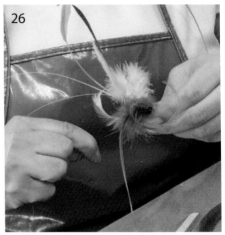

As the mount grows, a little more glue is added between bindings (27). The mount begins to look very attractive – see how the curled spiky goose feathers add depth and interest to the arrangement.

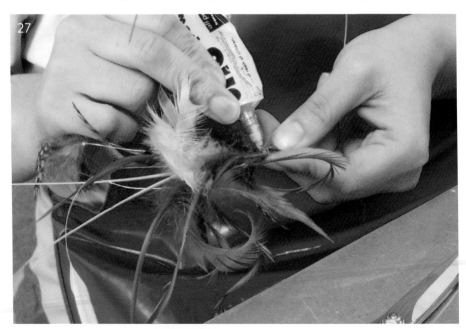

8. Finishing and using your mount

Once a mount has been finished, it can be fixed to a comb, a hair band, a small hat base or a hat. First, however, you may need to finish the mount neatly by covering the binding threads and any unsightly ends, even if it is going to be bound onto a hair band. Consider how much of the base of the mount will be seen before deciding if you need to finish it. Finishing can be done in several ways.

An attractive way to cover the end of the mount with its quills, wires and threads, is to sew up a small cone from silk or other toning fabric, and insert the quills and wires into this. When you are satisfied that it is the right shape and size, take it off and place dabs of hot melt glue onto the quills to be covered. Quickly insert them into the cone, and press the fabric in here and there, forming a pleasantly irregular shape which disguises the base of the mount. In the picture below (28), a toning silk cone beautifully finishes a mount of hackle and curled spiky goose feathers. This is an excellent way to finish a mount which will be in a more exposed position – as a trimming on a hat, for example.

28

If sinamay has featured in your mount, or if the fascinator is going to be used on a sinamay base, then a narrow bias strip of sinamay can be used to finish the mount. In figure 29 below, you can see how a slightly longer sinamay strip has been used to make a very simple hair adornment. The end of a bias strip of sinamay has been cut into a leaf-shape and the edges rolled. The remainder of the strip has been folded, rolled and wrapped around itself to make a long 'tube' which fits neatly along the top of a comb. A bias strip such as this can be used to finish any mount. Before the final fixing to comb or band, try the mount in your hair to see which way it is seen to best advantage. This will help you to see how it should be positioned on the comb or band. Stitch it in place or fix with hot melt glue. In figure 30 below, sinamay shapes and hackle feathers have been wrapped in a piece of bias sinamay and the whole mount attached to a small comb.

29
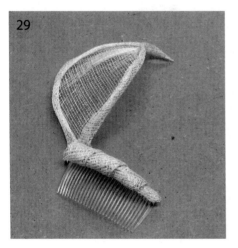

30

Mounts can also be used as trimmings or finishing touches for hats. In this case the mount will have been designed to complement the hat. However, a mount on a suitable base can form a delightful little hat in it's own right. In figure 31 we show some of the ready-made bases onto which a mount could be fixed.

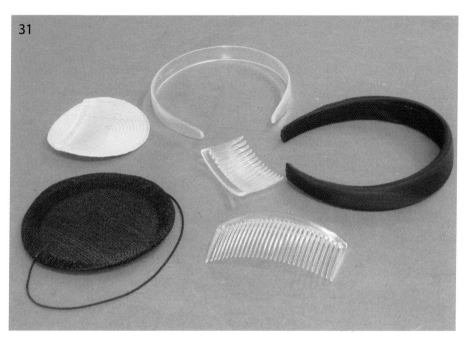

31

Clockwise from centre top: clear alice band; satin-covered, padded alice band; large comb (small comb in centre of picture); sinamay hat-base with elastic prong attached (basic colours only); stitched-straw hat base with comb attached (range of colours available). These last two are large enough to be a secure base for attaching a mount and yet small enough to be hidden beneath a mount, so that their colour is not critical.

If you wish to use your mount on a hair band, you will need to use silk or bias binding to finish the mount and to bind it to the band, as sinamay is too coarse for this. It might seem that finishing the mount first in this case is not necessary, but it is much easier to separate the process of finishing from that of binding, as it can be quite difficult to adequately cover the unsightly base of a mount at the same time as binding it to a hair band or comb. Before you begin work, check the position of the mount on the band, and mark where it is to be placed. Cut a 2 inch (5 cm) wide bias strip at least 1 ½ times the length of the hair band. Press a ½ inch (12mm) hem along one long side. Turn one end of the strip under. Put a little glue over the end of the hair band and neatly wrap the beginning of the bias strip around it, making sure any raw edges are covered as you wrap. Alter the angle of wrapping slightly, and continue gluing and wrapping up the hair band until you come to the place where the mount is to be positioned. Hold the mount in place on the band with a little glue, then wrap the bias strip around both band and mount. Keep checking that no raw edges are showing, and that the band and mount are both securely wrapped (32). Once the mount is in place, continue wrapping and glueing the band as before (33), making a neat glued finish at the other end.

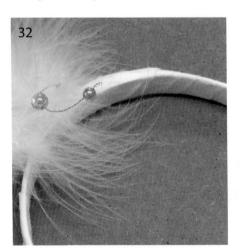

32

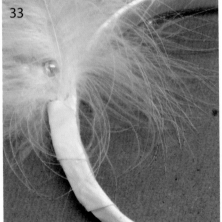

33

8. Creating a 'cocktail hat' base for your mount

Sometimes the best way to show off your mount is to add it to a hand-made hat base of the same colour as the mount. You can dye small amounts of sinamay and perhaps some ready-made sinamay flowers at the same time as you are dyeing feathers. Alternatively, you can create a base from any colour of sinamay and add your mount or other decorations to it. If you only have small pieces of sinamay, them you might want to dye some white satin bias binding as well.

Cover the polystyrene head with cling film (34). This will protect it and also prevent the blocked sinamay from sticking to it.

Smooth the cling film down (35). There is no need to pin it in place.

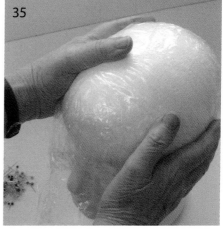

Cut three pieces of sinamay, approx 10 inches (25cm) square. If you are going to create a bias strip of sinamay for binding your base, then cut the squares from a corner of your sinamay piece, leaving as much material available on the bias as you can. Lay the squares as shown on your working surface and spray lightly with water (36).

Stand the head on an old towel on the table. This will protect the table from water and more importantly, from the glue which we will shortly be using. Pick the pieces up all together and lay them centrally over the prepared head. Put 2 pins in at one edge to hold them in place (37).

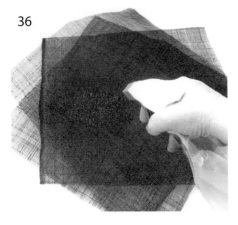

36

37

Smooth the sinamay over the head and pin the other side (38).

Spray again with water so that the sinamay is really wet, and repeat pinning as shown (39). Now the sinamay is held firmly in place over the head. Begin to pull down firmly

on the corners of the sinamay squares in turn, pinning as you go. Begin in one quarter and pull and pin until the sinamay in that quarter is smooth against the head. Repeat with the opposite quarter, then similarly with the other two.

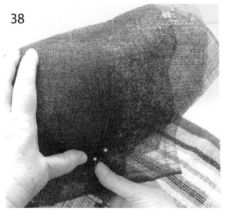

38

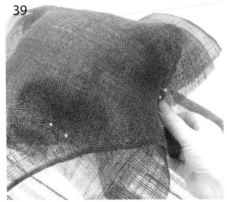

39

The sinamay should now conform to the shape of the top of the head as shown below (40). Small pleats and wrinkles between the pins don't matter as long as the main part is smooth. Spray again with water.

Make some stiffener by mixing one tablespoon of PVA Craft glue with six tablespoons of water in a small bowl. Stir well to ensure that there are no lumps. Brush this mixture liberally all over the wet sinamay (41). When you are sure that every part has been stiffened, put the head to dry. Standing in a warm room overnight will accomplish this.

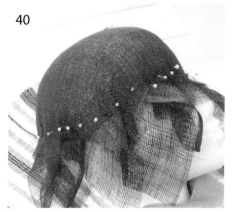

40

41

While the sinamay is drying, prepare the binding. Note: if you are using small pieces of sinamay and don't have sufficient to create a binding, you can use a ready-made bias binding or one cut from fabric such as silk.

To create a sinamay binding, mark a line on the diagonal on the fabric using the chinagraph pencil and long ruler. Measure and draw a second line 4 inches (10cm) away from and parallel to the first line. Cut out this long bias strip. Fold it in half longways and press with the iron. Open the strip out again and press each long side to the middle. Finally, fold the strip in half again. All the raw edges are now hidden, and the strip is ready to be used (42).

The strip is rather wide for the size of the piece, so make it narrower (and longer) by stretching it between your hands as shown over the page (43). It is easier to make a wide strip narrower by this method than it is to cut and fold a narrower strip – a point worth remembering!

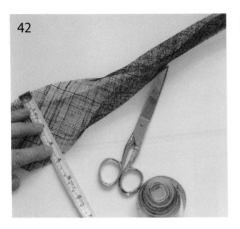

42

43

When the sinamay on the head is completely dry, use the pencil to mark the shapes of the pieces you want to make. A teardrop shape makes an attractive base (44). Position it where the point will fit into the lowest smooth part of the blocked sinamay. This will leave space for more sinamay shapes to be cut.

Here we show an oval marked

on the sinamay at the side of the head (45). And here is a small circle, marked between the other two shapes (46).

When you are happy with your designs, take out all the pins and gently ease the sinamay off the head. The cling film will come off with it, but it is easy to pull it away from the sinamay (47). Discard the cling film and cut out the shapes.

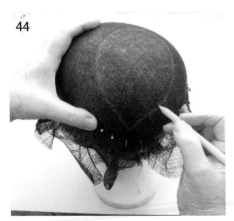

44

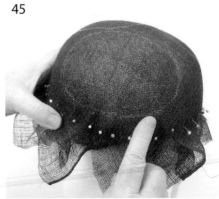

45

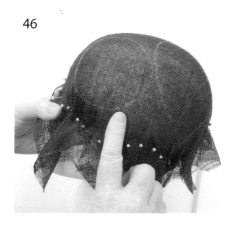

46

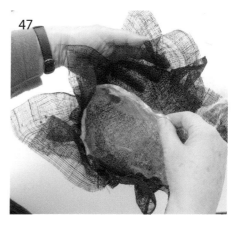

47

Use the pliers or wire cutters to cut a length of wire which will go round the tear-drop shape with approx 2 inches (5cm) overlap (48).

Draw the wire firmly between your finger and thumb to curve it to approximately the shape of the sinamay (49). Keep the curve as smooth as you can. Unintended sharp bends can be hard to get rid of!

Bend the angle for the point of the tear-drop with the pliers, positioning it so that the wire overlaps on one side of the tear-drop (50 & 51).

48

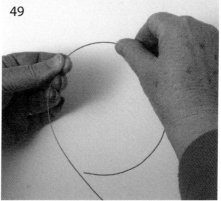

49

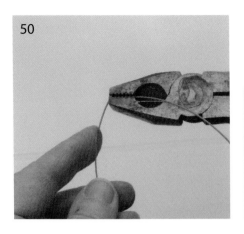

Thread the sewing machine with matching thread and set it to a wide zig-zag stitch with a short stitch length. With the concave side upwards, begin stitching at the side opposite the wire join and stitch the wire to the very edge of the sinamay (52). Sew slowly, being careful not to hit the wire with the needle. When you have stitched a few inches, check that the angle of the wire is still in the correct position to be sewn to the sinamay angle. If it isn't, then slide the wire through the stitching until it is (53).

The stitching is complete. The wire is held in place around the edge of the piece.

If you prefer to sew by hand, then use a doubled, knotted thread and a blanket stitch to sew the wire in place (54 & 55).

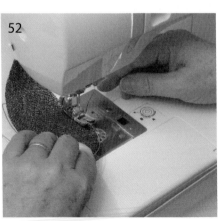

54

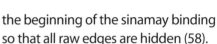

55

Take the binding you prepared earlier and place it over the edge of the wired sinamay. Because it is cut on the bias, it will conform easily to the curve as you smooth it round with your hands (56).

The join should come at the point of the teardrop, so ease the binding closely round and cut it to allow a 1 inch (2.5cm) overlap (57).

Turn the extra sinamay in neatly under

the beginning of the sinamay binding so that all raw edges are hidden (58).

If your machine has a variety of stitches, then we recommend choosing the 'three step zig-zag' stitch for stitching the binding in place. It will be almost invisible when sewn, as the stitching so closely conforms to the weave of the sinamay. However, you can use straight stitch if you are careful to keep it beautifully straight, or a zig-zag stitch.

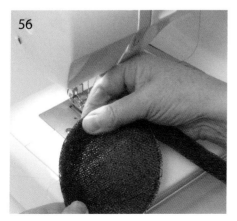

56

57

58

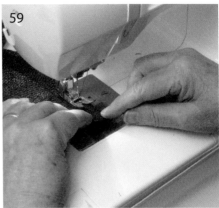

59

The binding is sewn neatly in place (59 and 60). We will demonstrate hand-sewing the binding as we work with the oval shape next.

Wire the edge of the oval shape just as you did the tear-drop, using hand or machine stitching. Take the remaining length of binding you created and open it as shown (61). Cut the binding at an angle, along the weave of the sinamay.

With the cut end at one long side, ease the binding round the shape as before (62).

If you are sewing it in place by hand, thread a needle with a doubled, knotted thread and use a backstitch to attach it to the oval, beginning to stitch just forward of the cut end (63). Keep your stitches small and even, and line them up with the weave of the sinamay for the most invisible result.

60

61

As you approach the point where you began stitching, cut the sinamay strip at the same angle as at the beginning so that the ends neatly overlap. Stitch in place and finish off securely (64). This oval will be attached to the tear drop, and will be the background for the feather mount you have created.

To show you other possibilities, this mount (65) was created from a group of feathers plus a purchased sinamay rose, some leaves and also some beaded stems. Having made up the mount, we disguised the ends of the wire with a binding of bias cut sinamay as described previously.

Place the finished mount within the concave side of the oval, positioning it so that it can be seen to advantage. You may need to curve the wire stems to conform to the dish of the oval. When you are happy, stitch it securely in place with a doubled, knotted thread (65).

Put the oval against the tear-drop, convex surfaces together and decide on the best position and angle. You may want to try it against your head or against the polystyrene head to check that you have it right. When you've made your choice, stitch it in place securely (66). Keep your stitches neat and as invisible as possible.

65

66

Finally, bind the comb with a narrow, matching ribbon, anchoring the end with a few small stitches. This not only makes the piece more attractive, it allows it to be sewn to the fascinator more easily (67).

Attach the bound comb to the underside of the teardrop, checking as you do so that the angle is right to hold the fascinator securely in the hair. You now have a beautiful finished piece!

Here is a similar piece which Beth has created from sinamay and bias binding dyed to the same colour as the feathers (68). She has added the mount which she created earlier, plus some ready-made sinamay flowers which were also dyed. See how attractive the completed fascinator looks! (69&70).

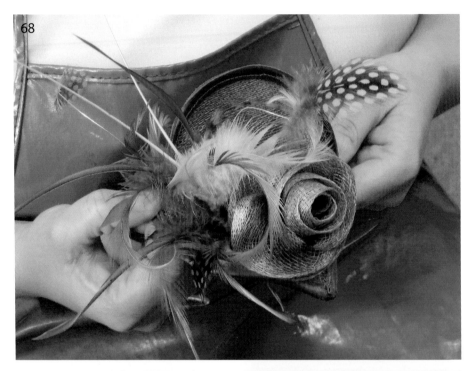
68

69

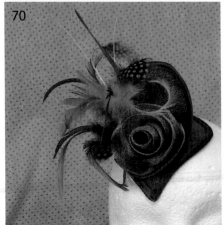
70

Model: Lara Forbes

40

If you want to add some veiling to a fascinator, here's how to do it: Cut the veiling as shown (71), trimming off any spiky ends. The piece shown is very small, just to show the angles at which to cut. The edge beside the left hand will form the curve around the face or brow. The three other edges will be gathered up into a bunch and will be sewn to the fascinator.

Here is a larger piece of veiling cut as shown previously, and gathered up ready to be sewn in position (72).

For this version (73) we use a smaller mount, comprising just a rose and leaf, to adorn the fascinator. The veiling plays a major role, and we don't want to detract from it. Stitch the gathered veiling neatly and securely to the mount.

Here we use a tear-drop alone as the base for the veiling and mount (74). Try it against your head for the best angle. When you have settled on the best position, stitch it securely to the base.

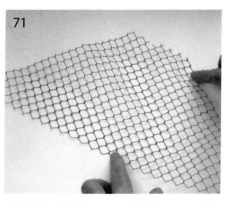

71

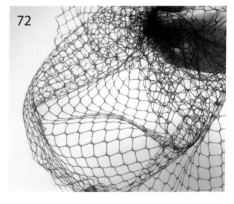

72

73

74

As before, bind the comb and attach it to the underside of the tear-drop (75).

Another lovely fascinator! (76). You still have a small circular shape of blocked sinamay to play with, so why not create another mount and make a further lovely piece?

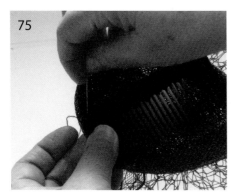

Some inspiration

We hope that you are now inspired to start dyeing and manipulating feathers to create wonderful and original mounts of your own!

'Fantasy Feathers' students at the Wombourne School of Millinery amazed us with their lovely creations. Our pictures show how the techniques described above can be used in very different ways.

Candy (left) created this corsage using sinamay leaves and a rose, spiky goose, guinea fowl and coq feathers. She attached a brooch pin, easily sewn or glued to the back of the corsage.

Christine (below) incorporated her dyed and manipulated feathers into this amazing coronet, created to wear at a photo shoot for the opening of a special event. The coronet also contains twisted chenille stems and pieces of handmade felt.

These two pieces by Edna Griffiths (below) and Linda Bratley (left) demonstrate the dramatic effects that can be achieved with feather mounts and very little else! Both elected to add feathers to both ends of their mounting wire. Edna's was converted into a wonderfully striking hat simply by adding a length of crin, which neatly encased the less interesting centre, while Linda's mount of curled natural pheasant feathers needed only a small feather 'flower' at the centre to turn it into a very exciting piece, full of movement and drama.

Juliette's blue head piece (below left) shows how dramatic even simple arrangements of feathers and sinamay can be. Sometimes, as the saying goes, 'less is more'! Notice how she has used beaded stems and dyed-to-match feathers within the sinamay 'lilies'. See also the neat sinamay binding which finishes the arrangement which is mounted on a comb.

A roll of random-dyed sinamay inspired Woody to create this starburst of orange (below right). She cut petal shapes from the sinamay and rolled the edges, then added several different kinds of feathers she had dyed in various toning shades.

Dee (below left) added this beautiful pink and black mount to a miniature topper in cream – a real wow of a combination! Bold mounts such as this one would also look wonderful on large brimmed hats of all kinds, making them truly original.

Olivia (below right) blocked two small sinamay shapes, bound them with matching petersham ribbon and mounted her pink and orange coq and spiky goose feather arrangement between them to make a really striking head piece.

Have you created a really special fascinator? If you'd like to send us a photo of your creation, we'll put it in our newsletter, and the best photos will be added to the inspiration section of this book when it gets reprinted.

Send images (high resolution please) to mail@how2hats.com with the subject line 'Fantastic Feathers fascinator'.

Anne (below top left) has created a white whirlpool by curling spiky goose feathers and mounting them onto a comb in a spiral form which is simple but very effective.

Finally, Beth (below bottom and right) models two of her own creations. The white one incorporates a turkey flat and coq feathers of different lengths, with some hackle feathers, combined into a lovely, gently curved piece which would be ideal for a bride. The second shows just how effective spiky goose feathers are when knotted. The gold and bronze feathers have a metallic look which ideally complements the barbed look of the knotted spikes.

We hope that these lovely pieces, which were not difficult to make, will inspire you to make wonderful creations of your own.

This book is available in hard copy and elctronic book (ebook) format.
Visit **www.how2hats.com** for these and many other titles.

11 Easy Projects for Hat Lovers

Classic Hat

Crin Hats (Horsehair)

How to make a double brimmed hat

Easy Sinamay Hats using Pre-formed Brims 1

Easy Sinamay Hats using Pre-formed Brims 2

Feathered Creations

Feathers, feathers, feathers

Felt Cloche Hat

Finishing touches

Finishing Touches 2

Freeform Felt Hats

Fresh flowers on hats

Hat Magic

Hints and Tips

How to make Men's hats

Setting up a millinery business

Millinery Materials

Profit from your Hats

How to make silk flowers

How to make a silk hat

Sinamay hat

Sinamay hat 2

How to make Stitched Strip Hats

Tiara Magic 1 with Janet Ricketts

Wild Hats

Wire Frame Hats